Visions of Tennis

Visions of Tennis

A CELEBRATION OF THE WORK OF
THE ALLSPORT PHOTOGRAPHIC AGENCY.
THE WORLD'S FINEST
TENNIS PHOTOGRAPHY.

Quiller Press

LONDON

First published in 1996 by
Quiller Press Ltd
46 Lillie Road
London SW6 1TN

A CIP catalogue record for this book
is available from the British Library

ISBN 1 899163 25 5

Editor: Henry Wancke
Editorial Contributors: Rod Laver, John Parsons,
Clive Brunskill, Gary M Prior, Henry Wancke
Project Director: James Nicholls

Designer and Picture Editor: Robert Kelland
Picture Research: Elaine Lobo

Produced by Mike Powell & Associates
Norfolk House, 57 Sandelswood End, Beaconsfield, Bucks HP9 2AA

Origination by Colour Origination Ltd, London
Printed in Italy by Rotolito Lombarda S.p.A.

Jim Courier, Australian Open, 1994 (half-title page)
PHOTOGRAPH BY CLIVE BRUNSKILL

Arantxa Sanchez Vicario, French Open, 1994 (frontispiece)
PHOTOGRAPH BY CLIVE BRUNSKILL

Boris Becker, Wimbledon, 1993 (title page)
PHOTOGRAPH BY CHRIS COLE

Michael Chang, French Open, 1994 (left)
PHOTOGRAPH BY CLIVE BRUNSKILL

INTRODUCTION

THE ESSENCE of great sports photography is to show the drama, excitement and emotion of the sport. *Visions of Tennis,* taken from the files of the Allsport photographic agency, brings together a selection of tennis images that encapsulate one of the most enduring and international of all games. A book that is as simple as its title, *Visions of Tennis* will hopefully lead its audience to a greater insight into the game, its traditions, characters and moments of outstanding beauty.

L'OBJECTIF de la photographie du sport de compétition est d'en révéler l'aspect dramatique, émotionnel et passionnant. L'ouvrage, *Visions of Tennis,* extrait des dossiers de l'agence de photographie Allsport, rassemble une sélection de photos de tennis qui résument l'histoire de l'un des sports les plus anciens et les plus adulés au monde. Cet ouvrage *Visions of Tennis,* est à la mesure de son titre, c'est-à-dire simple. Nous espérons, qu'il permettra aux lecteurs de mieux appréhender le jeu du tennis, ses traditions, ses personnages et ses moments exceptionnels de beauté.

BEI GUTER SPORTFOTOGRAFIE geht es im wesentlichen darum, die Dramatik, die Spannung und die emotionalen Momente des Sports einzufangen. Für *Visions of Tennis* wurde eine Auswahl von Tennisfotografien aus den Archiven der Allsports Fotoagentur zusammengestellt, die Impressionen einer der beständigsten und internationalsten Sportarten einfangen. *Visions of Tennis* – ein Buch, das so einfach ist wie sein Titel – möchte dem Betrachter tiefere Einblicke gewähren in den Sport selbst, seine Traditionen, seine Akteure und seine schönsten Momente.

LO QUE PRETENDEN las grandes fotografías de temas deportivos es mostrar todo el dramatismo, pasión y emoción del deporte. Estas *Visions of Tennis,* procedentes de los archivos de la agencia fotográfica Allsport, son una selección que define por sí misma uno de los juegos más internacionales y perdurables. *Visions of Tennis* es un libro tan sencillo como su título, que ayudará a sus lectores -al menos así lo esperamos- a comprender mejor este juego, sus tradiciones, sus personajes y su indudable belleza.

L'ESSENZA della grande fotografia degli sport consiste nel mostrare l'intensità, l'eccitazione e l'emozione dello sport. *Visions of Tennis* – proveniente dagli archivi dell'agenzia fotografica Allsport riunisce una selezione di immagini che infondono le emozioni di uno dei giochi di più lunga tradizione e maggior diffusione nel mondo. Un libro semplice come il suo titolo – *Visions of Tennis* – che speriamo possa coinvolgere il pubblico ad una maggiore comprensione del gioco, delle sue tradizioni, dei suoi protagonisti e dei suoi momenti di eccezionale fascino.

Karsten Braasch, Wimbledon, 1995

PHOTOGRAPH BY GARY M PRIOR

Jimmy Connors, Wimbledon, 1988

PHOTOGRAPH BY BOB MARTIN

FOREWORD

by Brian Tobin
President, International Tennis Federation

TENNIS HAS A MAGIC that few sports can provide. A mixture of drama and delight, of tension, skill and sunshine. It is no surprise that sports photographers enjoy the opportunities the game provides for eye-catching pictures.

Some of the best examples of the specialist art of tennis photography appear between the covers of this book and provide a wonderful record of the way the game has evolved over the years.

It should have a place on any tennis lover's bookshelves and I wish it every success.

LE TENNIS BÉNÉFICIE D'UNE MAGIE que peu de sports peuvent revendiquer. Cette magie résulte de l'association de moments dramatiques et heureux, de tension, d'habileté et de victoire. Rien de surprenant à ce que les photographes sportifs apprécient les opportunités de prendre des photos inédites.

Cet ouvrage contient quelques-unes des meilleures illustrations de l'art photographique du tennis, et reconstitue avec splendeur l'évolution de ce sport.

Visions of Tennis a sa place dans la bibliothèque de tout passionné de tennis, et je lui souhaite un énorme succès.

NUR WENIGE SPORTARTEN üben die gleiche Anziehungskraft aus wie Tennis – diese Mischung aus Dramatik und Vergnügen, Spannung, Geschicklichkeit und Sonnenschein. So ist es nicht verwunderlich, daß Sportfotografen die Vorzüge dieses Spiels gerne nutzen, um außergewöhnliche Fotos zu schießen.

Einige der besten Beispiele für die besondere Kunst der Tennisfotografie, die zugleich auch die Entwicklung des Spiels über die Jahrzehnte dokumentieren, finden sich in diesem Buch.

Ich hoffe deshalb, daß dieses Buch, das im Bücherregal keines Tennisliebhabers fehlen sollte, ein großer Erfolg werden wird.

EL TENIS TIENE UNA MAGIA difícil de encontrar en otros deportes. Una mezcla de emoción, placer, tensión, habilidad y tardes soleadas. No es ninguna sorpresa que los fotógrafos deportivos aprovechen las ocasiones que el

juego les proporciona para conseguir imágenes fascinantes.

Las tapas de este libro esconden algunos de los mejores ejemplos de este arte especializado que es la fotografía de tenis. Sus páginas recogen un magnífico registro de la evolución de este juego a lo largo de los años.

Creo que todos los amantes del tenis deberían hacerle un hueco en su biblioteca, y personalmente le auguro el mayor de los éxitos.

IL TENNIS HA UNA MAGIA comune a ben pochi sport. Un insieme di divertimento e sofferenza, di tensione, abilità e allegria. Non stupisce quindi il fatto che i fotografi sportivi colgano con piacere le opportunità che il gioco offre per scattare fotografie di forte impatto visivo.

Nelle pagine di questo volume compaiono alcuni dei migliori esempi della sofisticata arte della fotografia del gioco del tennis e visualizza una splendida testimonianza del modo in cui il gioco si è evoluto nel corso degli anni.

Auguro a questo libro di entrare a far parte delle librerie di tutti gli amanti del tennis.

Andre Agassi and Boris Becker, French Open, 1991
PHOTOGRAPH BY BOB MARTIN

LEGENDS

Rod Laver, Wimbledon, 1971

LEGENDS

by Rod Laver

LOOKING BACK it is amazing to think how much tennis has changed in my lifetime, not least the transition from an amateur sport, to a major commercial enterprise. As someone who came into the game long before prize money was common place – when playing Wimbledon and representing your country in the Davis Cup were what mattered most – I would pinpoint three factors which have been the most significant in leading us to where we are today.

First there was Open tennis. How much so many of us owe to Herman David (Wimbledon chairman at the time) for allowing professional players like myself, who had been out of major Championships for five years, to become eligible. I was then 30 but still capable of competing and therefore able to enjoy the best of both worlds.

Next there was the introduction of the tie-break, allowing television to truly introduce tennis as a major spectator sport. And more recently there has been the arrival of the composite racket technology, which has created tremendous interest and extra participation by making it easier for the masses who just want to play socially.

All we need to do now is make sure that talent does not become abused by too much technology.

LORSQUE JE FAIS UN RETOUR ARRIERE, je suis surpris de constater à quel point le tennis a changé. C'était au départ un sport d'amateurs, puis il a évolué et représente aujourd'hui une véritable entreprise commerciale. En tant que joueur qui s'est investi à une époque où l'argent n'était pas une finalité, où la participation au tournoi de Wimbledon et le fait de représenter son pays à la Coupe Davis étaient les seules motivations, je souhaiterais souligner trois facteurs qui ont le plus contribué à la situation actuelle du tennis.

Il y eu tout d'abord les Open de tennis. Nombre d'entre nous sommes redevables à Herman David (Président de Wimbledon, à l'époque) d'avoir permis aux joueurs professionnels qui n'avaient pas participé à d'importants championnats depuis cinq ans, et dont je faisais partie, de se qualifier.

J'avais alors 30 ans, et j'étais encore à même de participer à des compétitions, et par conséquent de profiter des meilleurs aspects des deux conceptions du tennis.

Plus tard, l'introduction du tie-break permit à la télévision de présenter le tennis comme un véritable sport de grand public. Plus récemment, l'introduction de la technologie des raquettes composite suscita un énorme intérêt auprès des joueurs du grand public et rendit ce sport plus accessible à ceux qui le pratiquent par plaisir.

Rod Laver, Ken Rosewall, Tony Roche and Tom Okker, London, 1969
("Legends", pages 12-13)

Aujourd'hui, nous devons veiller à ce que la technologie ne masque pas le talent.

RÜCKBLICKEND ist es doch erstaunlich, wie sehr sich der Tennissport über die Jahre und Jahrzehnte verändert hat, besonders wenn man seine Entwicklung von einer Amateursportart zu einem wichtigen Wirtschaftsfaktor betrachtet. Als jemand, der zu einer Zeit mit dem Sport anfing, als Preisgelder noch lange nicht an der Tagesordnung waren und eine Wimbledon-Teilnahme oder ein Platz im Davis Cup-Team, das das eigene Land repräsentierte, noch über alles gingen, würde ich drei Faktoren herausgreifen, die für die Entwicklung des Tennis, wie wir es heute kennen, am entscheidendsten waren.

Zum ersten wäre die Schaffung der „Offenen Meisterschaften" zu nennen. Viele von uns haben Herman David (dem damaligen Wimbledon-Vorsitzenden) eine Menge zu verdanken, der es Profispielern wie mir, die vorher fünf Jahre lang von den großen Meisterschaften ausgeschlossen waren, wieder ermöglichte, sich zu qualifizieren. Ich war damals zwar schon 30, aber immer noch in der Lage an Turnieren teilzunehmen und konnte so am meisten von dieser neuen Regelung profitieren.

Es folgte die Einführung des Tie-Break, die es dem Fernsehen ermöglichte, Tennis nun auch einem breiteren Publikum näherzubringen. Die nächste entscheidende Entwicklung jüngeren Datums ist der Tennisschläger aus Verbundstoffen, der ein enormes Interesse geschaffen und mehr Spieler gewonnen hat, da durch ihn das Tennisspielen für all jene erleichtert wurde, die einfach nur zum Spaß spielen wollen.

Nun müssen wir nur noch darauf achten, daß spielerisches Talent nicht von der Technik mißbraucht und in den Hintergrund gedrängt wird.

SI VUELVO LA VISTA ATRAS, lo que más me sorprende es ver cuánto ha cambiado el tenis en el curso de mi vida. De esos cambios, uno de los más importantes ha sido que un deporte para aficionados se ha convertido en una empresa comercial de gran envergadura. Desde mi punto de vista -el de un jugador que llegó al tenis mucho antes de que fueran habituales los premios en metálico, cuando lo único que nos importaba era jugar en Wimbledon y representar a nuestro país en la Copa Davis- subrayaría tres factores determinantes en la trayectoria que nos ha conducido a la situación actual:

Primero llegó el régimen "Abierto" de competición. Cuánto debemos muchos de nosotros a Herman David (que dirigía Wimbledon en aquella época) por permitir el acceso a este campeonato a tenistas profesionales que, como yo mismo, llevábamos cinco años excluidos de los campeonatos relevantes. Yo tenía entonces treinta años, pero mantenía un buen nivel de competición y logré disfrutar de lo mejor de ambos mundos.

Después vino la muerte súbita, que permitió a la televisión convertir al tenis en un auténtico espectáculo deportivo. Más recientemente los avances tecnológicos han permitido fabricar raquetas de composición mixta que han despertado un tremendo interés y han hecho aumentar el número de practicantes, dado que ahora el tenis resulta más fácil para las masas que buscan una actividad de ocio.

Ahora lo único que falta es asegurarse de que el exceso de tecnología no vaya en detrimento del talento.

GUARDANDO INDIETRO è sorprendente constatare quanto il tennis sia cambiato in questi anni, in particolare la trasformazione da sport amatoriale a vera e propria impresa commerciale. Ho gareggiato molto tempo prima che i premi in denaro fossero una consuetudine, quando giocare a Wimbledon e rappresentare il proprio paese nella Coppa Davis erano i momenti più importanti. Alla luce di queste mie esperienze vorrei evidenziare tre fatti significativi che a mio parere hanno condotto alla situazione attuale.

Innanzitutto gli Open di tennis. Io, che sono stato escluso per cinque anni dai più importanti Tornei, e tutta la categoria dei giocatori professionisti, dobbiamo moltissimo a Herman David (all'epoca Presidente di Wimbledon) che ci autorizzò a partecipare.

All'epoca ero già trentenne, ma ancora in grado di competere e di gareggiare con i migliori del mondo.

Un altro fatto importante è stata l'introduzione del tie-break con il quale la televisione ha reso il tennis uno degli sport più spettacolari. Più recentemente si è giunti ad una tecnologia composita della racchetta che ha creato enorme interesse e ha reso più facile il gioco per le masse incrementando notevolmente il numero dei giocatori dilettanti.

Oggi dobbiamo solo preoccuparci che un eccesso di tecnologia non porti un cattivo uso del talento.

.

'Rocket' Rod Laver is the first player to achieve the Grand Slam twice, first as an amateur (1962) and then as a professional (1969).

Martina Navratilova, US Open, 1989
PHOTOGRAPH BY SIMON BRUTY

*T*he traditions of tennis are built on the exploits of players who
have by means of their exceptional talents, become legends
in the game.

Jean Borotra, Wimbledon, 1935 (above)

Suzanne Lenglen, Wimbledon, 1924 (right)

Ce qui fait la tradition du tennis ce sont les exploits des joueurs devenus des légendes grâce à leur exceptionnel talent.

Fred Perry, Wimbledon, 1934

Die Tradition des Tennis basiert auf den Leistungen jener Spieler, die dank ihres außergewöhnlichen Talents zu Legenden dieses Sports wurden.

Miss Helen Wills and Mrs GW Wightman, Paris Olympics, 1924 (above)

Bobby Riggs, Wimbledon, 1939 (left)

Frank Shields, Wimbledon, 1931 (right)

Las tradiciones del tenis se levantan sobre las gestas de los jugadores a los que su excepcional talento ha convertido en mitos de este deporte.

Arthur Ashe, Wimbledon, 1970 (above)

Lew Hoad, Wimbledon, 1956 (right)

Le tradizioni del tennis si basano sulle imprese di giocatori che, grazie al loro eccezionale talento, sono diventati delle leggende.

Billie Jean King, Wimbledon, 1968 (left)
PHOTOGRAPH
ALLSPORT HISTORICAL COLLECTION
© HULTON DEUTSCH

John McEnroe, Wimbledon, 1984 (right)
PHOTOGRAPH BY STEVE POWELL

Martina Navratilova,
Wimbledon, 1994

Photograph by Bob Martin

THE BEAUTIFUL GAME

Henri Leconte, Wimbledon, 1991

PHOTOGRAPH BY BOB MARTIN

THE BEAUTIFUL GAME

by Gary M Prior

FRANCE'S CHIC SUZANNE LENGLEN was noted in the twenties for her graceful on-court movement which was often described as balletic. Her elegance however, did not prevent her becoming an all-conquering all-time great, emerging recently as the player Monica Seles would most like to try and emulate. Seles's style cannot compare with the legendary Lenglen but off-court, the former Yugoslav certainly tried hard to bring back those fashions best associated with the roaring-twenties!

But beauty is in the eye of the beholder and whilst a certain amount of elegance left the game when women discarded tennis dresses in favour of more workman-like clothing, the change itself brought in a mass of exciting colour. From a different perspective the attractive tactical chess-like play of the post war competition was replaced by the raw ruggedness of today's speedy but power-based game.

A lot of the game's beauty is lost on spectators who can only marvel at the prowess of their heroes and heroines, but those who watch play in the lengthening shadows of a balmy summer evening at Wimbledon, are aware of the sensuous charm their sport can engender.

L'ÉLÉGANTE FRANÇAISE SUZANNE LENGLEN s'est distinguée dans les années 20 de par ses mouvements grâcieux sur les courts, ce qui lui valut d'être souvent comparée à une ballerine. Cependant, son élégance ne l'empêcha pas de devenir la meilleure joueuse de tous les temps. La joueuse Monica Seles a tenté ardemment de l'égaler. Le style de Seles ne peut être comparé à celui de la légendaire Lenglen mais, en dehors des courts, l'ex-Yougoslave a sans doute tenté de tout son coeur de faire revivre les belles manières caractérisant les trépidantes années 20!

Lorsque les tenues de style masculin ont remplacé les jupes, les joueuses ont perdu de leur élégance; ce changement de tenue a autorisé sur les courts des couleurs saisissantes. A la subtile technique de jeu qui était proche de celle des joueurs d'échecs durant la période d'après-guerre, s'est substituée une technique rude basée sur la puissance et la vitesse.

Les spectateurs ne savent pas apprécier le jeu dans toute sa splendeur, ils ne s'émerveillent que devant les prouesses de leurs héros et héroïnes. Par contre, ceux qui assistent à des matches durant les langoureux soirs d'été à Wimbledon, sont concients du charme sensuel que ce sport peut engendrer.

Stefan Edberg, Monte Carlo, 1994
("The Beautiful Game", pages 30-31)
PHOTOGRAPH BY CLIVE BRUNSKILL

SUZANNE LENGLEN, DIE SCHICKE FRANZÖSIN, machte in den zwanziger Jahren durch ihre graziösen, geradezu ballettartigen, Bewegungen auf dem Platz von sich reden. Bei aller Eleganz wurde sie aber auch eine der erfolgreichsten Spielerinnen aller Zeiten, der heute wohl Monica Seles am stärksten nacheifert. Sind Monica Seles und die legendäre Lenglen in ihrer Spielart auch nicht miteinander zu vergleichen, so versucht die ehemals für Jugoslawien spielende Seles doch, die Mode und Eigenheiten wieder zurückzubringen, die so gerne mit den „Roaring Twenties" in Verbindung gebracht werden.

Da aber auch im Tennissport die Devise gilt: „Schön ist was gefällt", brachte ein gewisser Verlust an Eleganz im Damentennis andererseits einen Gewinn an Farbe mit sich, als die Damen ihre Tenniskleider gegen etwas praktischere Kleidungsstücke eintauschten. Zum anderen wurde aber die attraktive, taktierende, fast schachartige Spielweise der Nachkriegszeit durch das direktere, schnellere und kraftbetontere Spiel der Gegenwart abgelöst.

Die ganze Schönheit und Ästhetik des Spiels offenbart sich allerdings kaum jenen Zuschauern, die nur über die Leistungen ihrer Heldinnen und Helden staunen wollen, wohl aber denen, die den länger werdenden Schatten an einem lauen Sommerabend in Wimbledon folgen und etwas von dem sinnlichen Reiz spüren, der diesem Spiel eigen ist.

LA ELEGANTE JUGADORA FRANCESA SUZANNE LENGLEN fue famosa en los años veinte por su forma de jugar, con movimientos tan fluidos que a menudo se comparaban con los del ballet. Sin embargo, su precioso estilo no le impidió convertirse en una de las grandes campeonas de todos los tiempos, conquistar todos los grandes trofeos e, incluso, saltar recientemente a las páginas de los periódicos como la jugadora a la que Mónica Seles desearía parecerse. No es posible comparar el estilo de Seles con el de la mítica Lenglen, pero no cabe duda de que fuera de la pista la ex-yugoslava ha intentado por todos los medios revivir las modas que todos asociamos con los locos años veinte.

Pero la belleza está en la mirada del que mira y, si bien es cierto que cuando las mujeres sustituyeron sus vestidos de tenis por prendas más prácticas desapareció de la pista un toque de elegancia, también lo es que el cambio trajo consigo una oleada de intenso colorido. Desde una perspectiva diferente, el atractivo juego táctico, ajedrecístico, que caracterizaba a esta competición en el período de posguerra fue sustituido por la dureza del juego actual, rápido pero basado fundamentalmente en la potencia.

Gran parte de la belleza del juego está vedada a aquellos espectadores que únicamente son capaces de apreciar las proezas de sus héroes y heroínas, pero los que contemplan apaciblemente el partido en Wimbledon mientras se extienden las sombras, en un suave atardecer de verano, son plenamente conscientes de la sensual atracción que suscita este deporte.

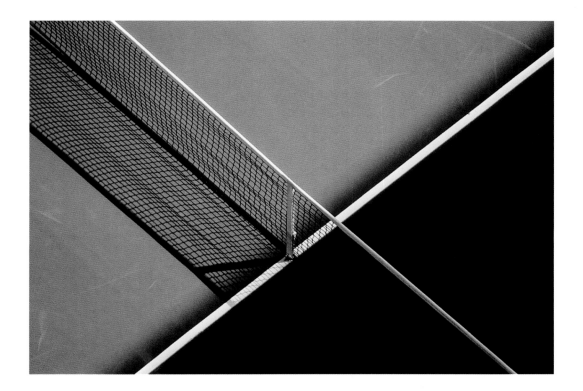

LA GRAZIOSA FRANCESE SUZANNE LENGLEN era conosciuta negli anni venti per i suoi armoniosi movimenti sul campo, spesso paragonati ad una danza. La sua eleganza non le impedì tuttavia di diventare imbattibile, una grande finora insuperata, che la giocatrice Monica Seles sta ultimamente cercando di emulare. Lo stile della Seles non è paragonabile a quello della leggendaria Lenglen, ma fuori dal campo l'ex-jugoslava ha certamente tentato di far rivivere quell' impronta degli anni ruggenti.

Ma in fatto di bellezza ognuno ha i suoi gusti e se il gioco ha certamente perso in eleganza quando le donne hanno abbandonato il femminile gonnellino in favore di un abbigliamento che ricorda le tute da lavoro, il cambiamento ha portato con sé una quantità di eccitanti colori. Osservando il fenomeno da una diversa prospettiva, la tecnica di gioco del dopoguerra, tatticamente interessante come gli scacchi, èstata sostituita dalla rudezza del gioco attuale, più veloce, e basato sulla potenza.

Gli spettatori che riescono a emozionarsi solo dinanzi alle prodezze dei loro eroi ed eroine perdono molto della bellezza del gioco. Ma gli spettatori di una partita giocata nelle ombre che sempre più si allungano in una mite serata estiva a Wimbledon sono ben consapevoli del fascino sensuale che il loro sport preferito può suscitare.

Gary M Prior is a staff photographer
for Allsport Photographic

Net detail, US Open
PHOTOGRAPH BY GARY M PRIOR

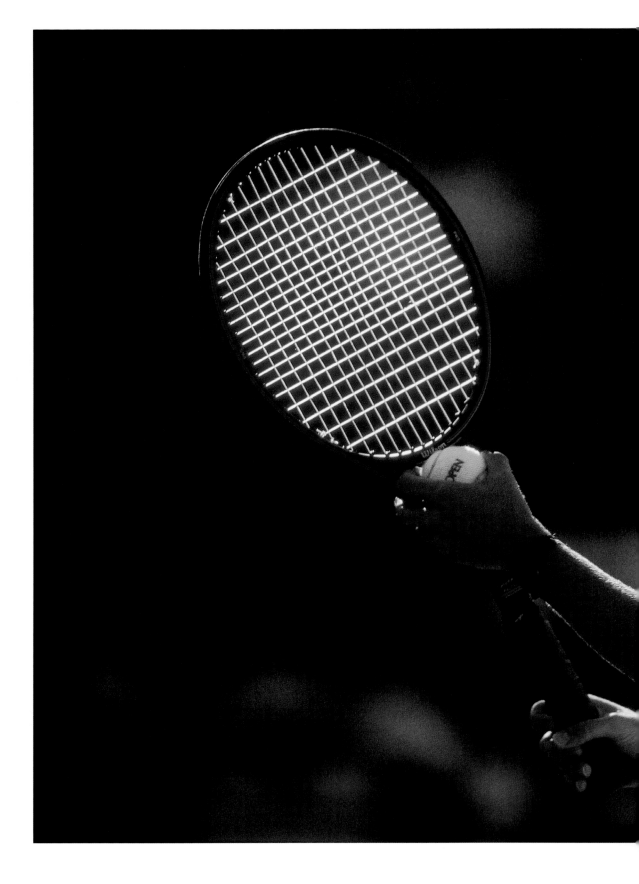

The imagery of the game is part of its great international appeal, with exciting characters, individual styles, colourful outfits and exotic venues.

Les images illustrant le jeu de tennis dégagent un charme extraordinaire au niveau international, de par la qualité des individus qui le caractérisent, de par le style individuel de chaque joueur, et de par l'esthétique des tenues colorées et des lieux de rencontre exotiques.

Mary Pierce,
US Open, 1994

PHOTOGRAPH BY GARY M PRIOR

Zur starken internationalen Anziehungskraft des Tennissports trägt auch die visuelle Vielfalt, d. h. schillernde Akteure, individuelle Stile, farbenfrohe Kleidung und exotische Austragungsorte bei.

**Kathy Jordan and Meredith McGrath,
French Open, 1991** (above)
PHOTOGRAPH BY CHRIS COLE

Anna Kournikova, Wimbledon, 1994 (right)
PHOTOGRAPH BY GARY M PRIOR

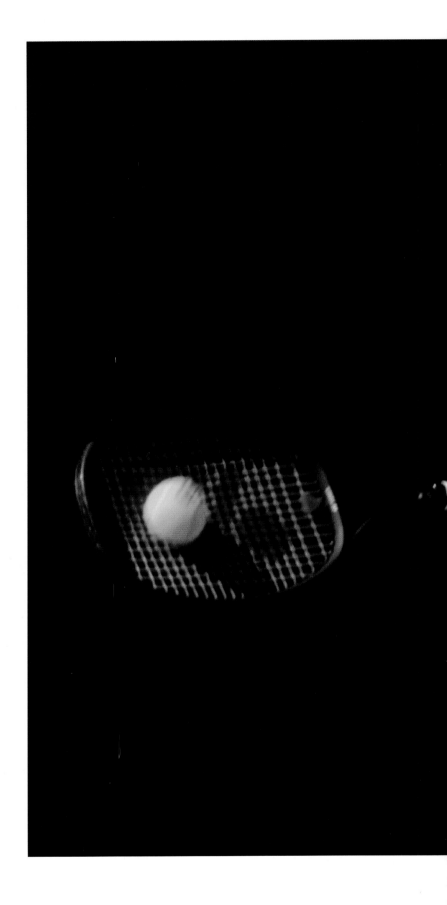

La imagen del juego forma parte de su gran atractivo internacional, con personajes apasionantes, estilos individuales, atuendos llenos de color y emplazamientos exóticos.

Mary Pierce, US Open, 1994 (above left)

Mary Pierce, Wimbledon 1995 (above right)

Photographs by Clive Brunskill

Lo scenario che il gioco scatena è parte integrante della grande attrattiva che suscita in tutto il mondo, con i suoi stimolanti protagonisti, i vari stili di gioco, l'abbigliamento coloratissimo e le località esotiche.

Steffi Graf, US Open, 1994 (above left)

Steffi Graf, French Open, 1994 (above right)

PHOTOGRAPHS BY CLIVE BRUNSKILL

*F*lowing movement and the symmetry of style
provides photographers with excellent
opportunities to capture the grace of the game.

Michael Chang, French Open, 1994
PHOTOGRAPH BY CLIVE BRUNSKILL

42 VISIONS OF TENNIS

*L*es mouvements harmonieux et le style symétrique du tennis offrent
d'excellentes occasions aux photographes de reproduire la grâce de ce jeu.

Steffi Graf, Australian Open, 1993 (left)
PHOTOGRAPH BY SIMON BRUTY

Stefan Edberg, US Open, 1991 (above)
PHOTOGRAPH BY ALLSPORT

Fließende Bewegungen und die stilistische Symmetrie erlauben es dem Fotografen auf einzigartige Weise, die Eleganz des Spiels festzuhalten.

Gabriela Sabatini, Key Biscayne, 1995 (left)

Natasha Zvereva, Australian Open, 1995 (above)

Photographs by Clive Brunskill

La fluidez del movimiento y la simetría del estilo proporcionan a los fotógrafos excelentes ocasiones de captar la belleza de este juego.

**Martina Hingis,
French Open, 1995**

Photograph by Clive Brunskill

I movimenti fluidi e la simmetria dello stile forniscono ai fotografi eccellenti opportunità per catturare la grazia del gioco.

Mary Joe Fernandez, Eastbourne, 1991 (left)
<small>PHOTOGRAPH BY RUSSELL CHEYNE</small>

Gabriela Sabatini, French Open, 1995 (above left)

Michael Chang, French Open, 1994 (above right)
<small>PHOTOGRAPHS BY CLIVE BRUNSKILL</small>

John McEnroe, US Open, 1989 (left)
PHOTOGRAPH BY SIMON BRUTY

Andre Agassi, Wimbledon, 1991 (right)
PHOTOGRAPH BY BOB MARTIN

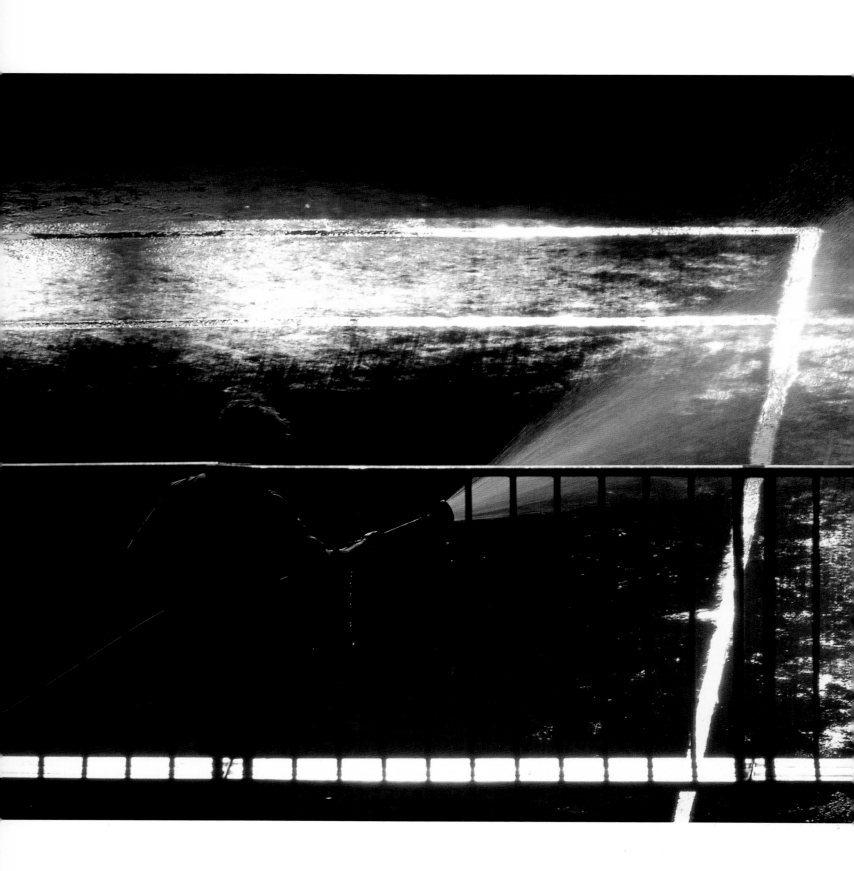

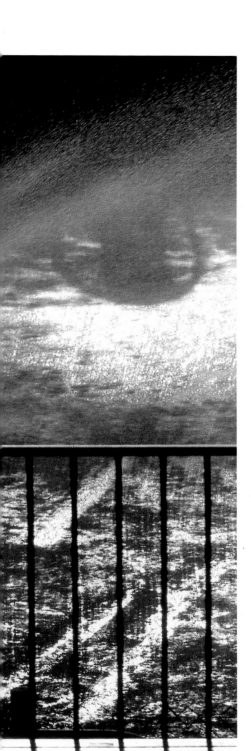

*R*ain or shine, the colour and the backdrops enhance the appeal of a truly exciting sport.

Wet court,
French Open, 1995, (left)
PHOTOGRAPH BY CLIVE BRUNSKILL

Spectators,
Wimbledon, 1991(right)
PHOTOGRAPH BY SIMON BRUTY

*Qu'il fasse beau ou qu'il pleuve, les couleurs
et les toiles de fond optimisent le charme
de ce sport si passionnant.*

Gabriela Sabatini, Liptons, 1994 (far left)

Key Biscayne silhouette, 1994 (left)

PHOTOGRAPHS BY SIMON BRUTY

Gigi Fernandez, Wimbledon, 1994 (above)

PHOTOGRAPH BY CLIVE BRUNSKILL

*Ob im Regen oder bei Sonnenschein –
die Farben und die Kulisse verstärken stets
den Reiz eines wirklich aufregenden Sports.*

Dusk, US Open, 1995 (above)
PHOTOGRAPH BY SIMON BRUTY

**Stefan Edberg v Thomas Muster,
Monte Carlo, 1994** (right)
PHOTOGRAPH BY CLIVE BRUNSKILL

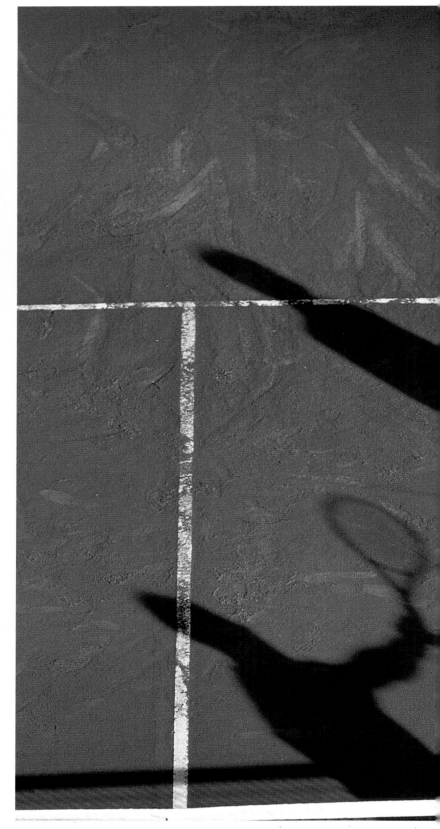

Llueva o haga sol, el color y el ambiente acentúan el atractivo de un deporte apasionante.

Leonardo Lavalle, Wimbledon, 1992 (top left)

Stefan Edberg, Wimbledon, 1993 (lower left)

Marcelo Rios, Wimbledon, 1995 (top right)

PHOTOGRAPHS BY GARY M PRIOR

Jim Courier, US Open, 1995 (lower right)

PHOTOGRAPH BY SIMON BRUTY

Pioggia o sole, i colori e gli scenari aumentano ulteriormente il fascino di uno sport veramente emozionante.

Gabriela Sabatini, Australian Open, 1995

PHOTOGRAPH BY CLIVE BRUNSKILL

Andre Agassi,
Wimbledon, 1995

Photograph by Clive Brunskill

Andre Agassi in action, 1989 - 1996

PHOTOGRAPHS BY BOB MARTIN, DAN SMITH, CLIVE BRUNSKILL,

THE GRAND SLAMS

Pete Sampras, US Open, 1993

Photograph by Simon Bruty

THE GRAND SLAMS

by John Parsons

THE FOUR GRAND SLAM tournaments, with Wimbledon, of course, the best known and most envied of them all, are undoubtedly the most precious and priceless jewels in the world of tennis.

When these events are taking place, even those whose sporting interests principally lie elsewhere, sit up and take notice.

Apart from bringing together the 128 best men and women players in the world for two weeks of wonderful competition, during which pride and performance matters even more than prize money, they excitingly reflect the varied character and culture of the nations in which they are staged.

The Australian Open's new home in Flinders Park, Melbourne, is a shining example of a vibrant, modern way of life which befits what is basically still a young country. At Roland Garros the Square of the Musketeers, with those evocative action-style statues of Messrs Borotra, Brugnon, Cochet and Lacoste contributes an artistic flavour, as important to Parisians as a gourmet lunch.

New York's Flushing Meadows is as wonderfully brash, noisy and unashamedly commercial as Wimbledon likes to appear low key and joyously traditional. Above all, individually and collectively, they are supreme.

LES QUATRE TOURNOIS DU GRAND CHELEM représentent, avec Wimbledon qui est bien entendu le plus connu et le plus convoité, les joyaux les plus précieux et les plus inestimables du monde du tennis.

Lorsque ces événements ont lieu, même ceux qui ont une préférence sportive éloignée du tennis ont plaisir à observer et analyser les jeux.

Ces tournois ne sont pas simplement l'occasion de rassembler les 128 meilleurs joueurs et joueuses du monde entier pour une compétition sportive extraordinaire deux semaines durant, et au cours de laquelle l'honneur et la performance comptent bien plus que l'argent en jeu. Ces tournois reflètent également la diversité des particularités et des cultures des nations qui les accueillent.

La nouvelle terre d'accueil de l'Open d'Australie, Flinders Park à Melbourne, est l'illustration brillante d'un mode de vie moderne et trépidant qui convient à ce pays encore jeune. A Roland Garros, la Place des Mousquetaires, avec ses statues dont le style évoque Messieurs Borotra, Brugnon, Cochet et Lacoste apporte une touche artistique aussi délicieuse que pourrait l'être un repas gourmet dégusté par les Parisiens.

Flushing Meadows à New York est aussi merveilleusement impétueux, bruyant et effrontément commercial que Wimbledon

Kenneth Carlsen, French Open, 1993
("The Grand Slams", pages 64-65)
PHOTOGRAPH BY SIMON BRUTY

aime à paraître discret et joyeusement traditionnel. Mais ils sont avant tout, du niveau
individuel et collectif suprêmes.

Die vier Grand Slam Turniere, zu denen
selbstverständlich auch Wimbledon zählt, sind
die bekanntesten und wahrscheinlich auch am
härtesten umkämpften Turniere, mit
Sicherheit aber die wertvollsten Edelsteine in
der Tenniswelt.

Bei diesen Ereignissen werden selbst
jene auf den Tennissport aufmerksam, deren
sportliche Interessen ansonsten eher in anderen
Bereichen liegen.

Diese Turniere bringen nicht nur die
128 besten Spieler und Spielerinnen aus aller
Welt für zwei Wochen zu hervorragenden
Spielen zusammen, in denen Stolz und
Leistungen sogar noch mehr gelten als
Preisgelder, sie spiegeln auch immer auf
außergewöhnliche Weise den Charakter und
die Kultur der Länder wider, in denen sie aus-
gerichtet werden.

So ist der Flinders Park in Melbourne,
die neue Austragungsstätte der Australian
Open, ein ausgezeichnetes Beispiel für den
pulsierenden, modernen Lebensstil, der so gut
zu diesem noch relativ jungen Land paßt. Im
Stadion Roland Garros schafft der „Platz der
Musketiere" mit seinen aus dem Leben gegriff-
enen, Erinnerungen weckenden Statuen der
Herren Borotra, Brugnon, Cochet und Lacoste
eine leicht künstlerische Atmosphäre, die für
die Pariser ebenso wichtig ist, wie ein
gepflegtes Mittagessen.

New Yorks Flushing Meadows ist
ebenso schrill, laut und schamlos kommerziell
wie Wimbledon sich gerne zurückhaltend und
heiter traditionell gibt. Vor allem aber sind

diese Turniere einfach unvergleichlich, einzeln
wie auch gemeinsam.

Los cuatro torneos que componen el
Grand Slam son, sin lugar a duda, las piedras
preciosas del mundo del tenis y, entre ellos,
Wimbledon es el más conocido y envidiado.

Estos acontecimientos son seguidos
atentamente incluso por personas que se sien-
ten interesadas principalmente por otros
deportes.

Además de reunir a los 128 mejores
jugadores y jugadoras del mundo durante dos
magníficas semanas de competición en las que
los tenistas valoran más el amor propio y la cal-
idad de su actuación que los premios en
metálico, estos acontecimientos ofrecen un
vibrante reflejo de la diversidad de caracteres y
culturas de los países en los que se desarrollan.

Las pistas de Flinders Park de
Melbourne, nueva sede del Abierto de
Australia, son un ejemplo del estilo de vida
vibrante y moderno de este país que sigue
siendo, en lo fundamental, un país joven. En
Roland Garros, las estatuas de la Plaza de los
Mosqueteros evocan el juego de Borotra,
Brugnon, Cochet y Lacoste, y ponen ese toque
artístico tan importante para los parisinos
como un almuerzo en un restaurante de lujo.

Flushing Meadows, en Nueva York
resulta deliciosamente insolente, ruidoso y
descaradamente comercial, del mismo modo
que Wimbledon opta por la discreción y el
amor a las tradiciones. Pero por encima de
todo, todos ellos, tanto individual como colec-
tivamente, constituyen la cima de este deporte.

I QUATTRO TORNEI DEL GRANDE SLAM, dei quali Wimbledon è naturalmente il più conosciuto ed ambito, sono indubbiamente il traguardo più prezioso e di valore inestimabile nel mondo del tennis.

In occasione di questi eventi, anche chi non ha un particolare interesse per il tennis si mette comodo e guarda.

Questi tornei non solo riuniscono i 128 migliori giocatori e giocatrici del mondo per due settimane di splendida competizione, durante le quali l'orgoglio e il risultato sportivo contano più del premio in denaro, ma rispecchiano in modo eccitante le varie caratteristiche e culture dei Paesi che li ospitano.

La nuova sede di Flinders Park, a Melbourne, in cui si svolgono gli Open d'Australia, è un eccellente esempio di uno stile di vita moderno e stimolante che si adatta perfettamente a quello che è un paese ancora giovane. Al Roland Garros le statue dei "Moschettieri" Borotra, Brugnon, Cochet e Lacoste così espressive, aggiungono quel tocco artistico così importante per i Parigini quanto un pranzo da gourmet.

Flushing Meadows a New York è splendidamente esuberante, rumoroso e spudoratamente commerciale quanto invece a Wimbledon piace essere sottotono e gioiosamente tradizionale. In ogni caso sono tutte affascinanti localita!

John Parsons is Lawn Tennis Correspondent for The Daily Telegraph

US Open, 1993

PHOTOGRAPH BY SIMON BRUTY

Australian Open

The yearly Grand Slam campaigns begin every January down under at the Australian Open, now staged in the most modern of venues at Flinders Park, Melbourne, on a cushioned acrylic court selected by the players in the late eighties.

Australian Open, 1995

PHOTOGRAPH BY CLIVE BRUNSKILL

Les campagnes annuelles du Grand Chelem commencent en janvier par l'Open d'Australie, qui est à présent organisé sur le site le plus moderne de Flinders Park, à Melbourne, sur un court en surface synthétique choisi par les joueurs à la fin des années 80.

*J*edes Jahr im Januar
beginnt der Grand Slam
in „Down Under" mit
den Australian Open,
die nun im modernen
Flinders Park in
Melbourne auf einem
gefederten Kunststoffbelag
ausgetragen werden, den
die Spieler in den späten
Achtzigern aussuchten.

**Mary Pierce,
Australian Open, 1995**

Photographs by Clive Brunskill

*L*a temporada anual del Grand Slam comienza en enero con
el Abierto de Australia, que actualmente se celebra en
las modernísimas instalaciones del Flinders Park de Melbourne,
sobre una pista acrílica amortiguadora elegida por los jugadores
a finales de los años ochenta.

Australian Open, 1995 (above)
PHOTOGRAPH BY GARY M PRIOR

Jim Courier, Australian Open 1993, (left)
PHOTOGRAPH BY SIMON BRUTY

*I grandi appuntamenti del Grande Slam iniziano ogni anno a gennaio con
gli Open d'Australia, ora ospitati nei modernissimi campi di Flinders Park
a Melbourne, su un campo sintetico prescelto dai giocatori
alla fine degli anni ottanta.*

Pete Sampras, Australian Open, 1994 (above left)
PHOTOGRAPH BY CLIVE BRUNSKILL

Steffi Graf, Australian Open, 1993 (above centre)

Ivan Lendl, Australian Open, 1991 (above right)
PHOTOGRAPHS BY SIMON BRUTY

Goran Ivanisevic, Australian Open, 1994 (right)
PHOTOGRAPH BY CLIVE BRUNSKILL

Roland Garros

*T*he French Open,
or Roland Garros,
represents the pinnacle
of clay court tennis where
a player's stamina and
dexterity are always tested
to the full.

Jay Berger,
French Open, 1989
PHOTOGRAPH BY SIMON BRUTY

L'Open de France ou Roland Garros représentent l'apogée du tennis sur terre battue où l'endurance et la dextérité d'un joueur sont toujours soumises à rude épreuve.

Thomas Muster,
French Open, 1995
(right)

Thomas Muster, 1995
(left below)
PHOTOGRAPHS BY CLIVE BRUNSKILL

Thomas Muster,
French Open, 1995
(left above)
PHOTOGRAPH BY SIMON BRUTY

Die French Open, oder besser gesagt das Stadion Roland Garros, sind der jährliche Höhepunkt des Sandplatztennis, bei dem stets die gesamte Kondition und Geschicklichkeit eines Spielers gefordert sind.

Gigi Fernandez, French Open, 1992 (above)
PHOTOGRAPH BY CHRIS COLE

Arantxa Sanchez Vicario, French Open, 1994 (right)
PHOTOGRAPH BY GARY M PRIOR

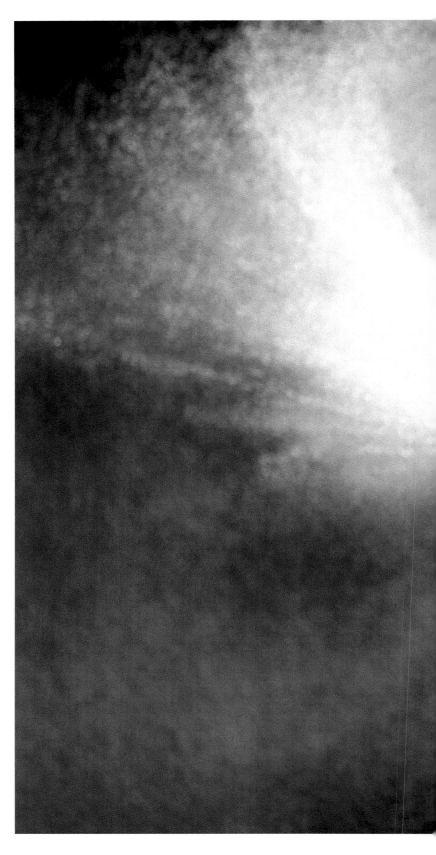

El Abierto de Francia, también conocido como "Roland Garros," es la cumbre del tenis sobre tierra batida, donde se ponen a prueba la resistencia física y la destreza del tenista.

Pat Cash, French Open, 1988 (top)

Ball detail (above)

Preparing the court, French Open, 1994 (right)

Gli Open di Francia al Roland Garros rappresentano il top del tennis su terra battuta dove la resistenza e l'abilità di ogni giocatore sono sempre messi alla prova ai massimi livelli.

Veronika Martinek, French Open, 1995 (left)
PHOTOGRAPH BY CLIVE BRUNSKILL

Ball-girl, French Open, 1994 (above)
PHOTOGRAPH BY GARY M PRIOR

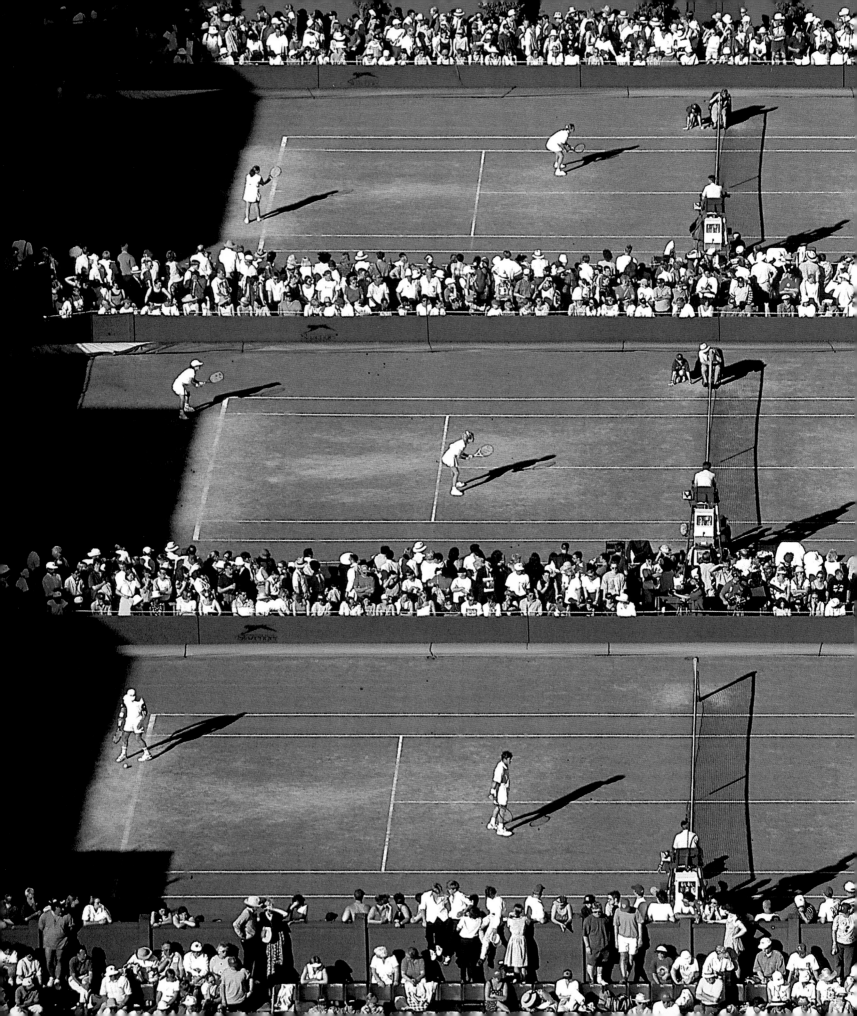

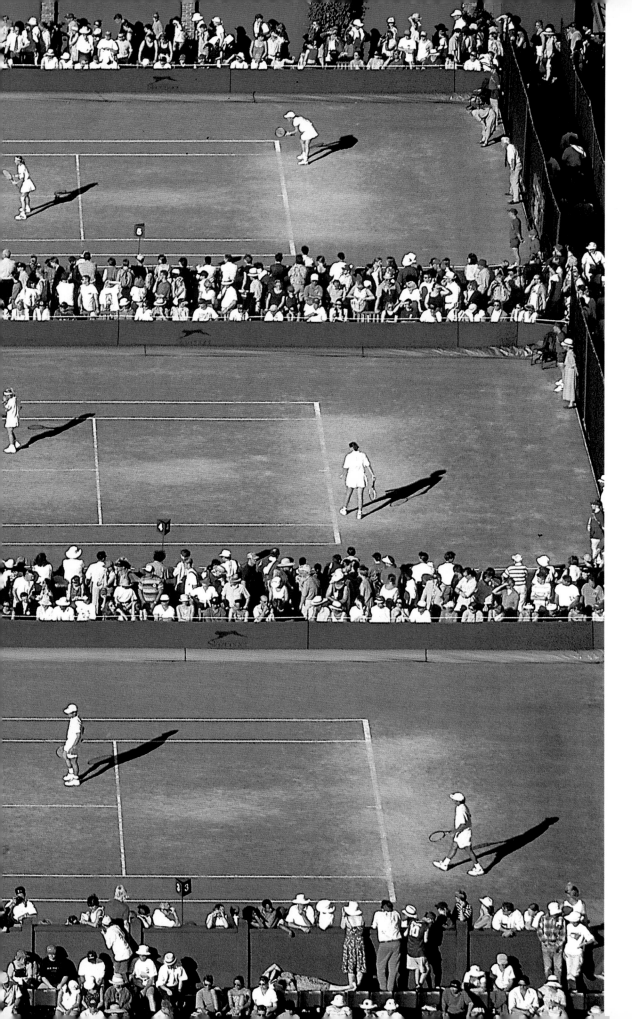

Wimbledon

*T*he Championships, the
most conventional of the
four majors, sticks
steadfastly to the surface
the game originated on,
maintaining immaculate
grass courts to ensure the
traditional English
Garden Party atmosphere
of 1877, continues.

Wimbledon, 1995
PHOTOGRAPH BY MIKE COOPER

*Le Championnat le plus conventionnel des quatre principaux
événements reste résolument fidèle à la surface sur laquelle
le jeu du tennis a pris naissance, en conservant les courts
en gazon intacts, afin de s'assurer que la traditionnelle
atmosphère des garden-parties anglaises de 1877 se perpétue.*

John McEnroe, Wimbledon, 1992 (left)
PHOTOGRAPH BY CHRIS COLE

Rain at Wimbledon, 1985, (above)
PHOTOGRAPH BY STEVE POWELL

*B*ei den All English Championships, dem konventionellsten der

"Großen Vier", hält
man beständig an dem
Belag fest, auf dem das
Spiel entstand, um mit
makellos gepflegten
Rasenplätzen die
Atmosphäre der
traditionellen englischen
"Garden Party" von 1877
immer neu aufleben
zu lassen.

**Michael Stich
v Boris Becker,
Wimbledon, 1991** (left)
PHOTOGRAPH BY RUSSELL CHEYNE

**Michael Stich,
Wimbledon, 1991** (right)
PHOTOGRAPH BY BOB MARTIN

El torneo de Wimbledon es el más convencional de los cuatro grandes. Permanece fiel a la superficie sobre la que se desarrolló el juego originalmente, y mantiene pistas de hierba inmaculada que ayudan a evocar el ambiente de lo que pudo ser una reunión inglesa al aire libre hacia 1877.

Andre Agassi, Wimbledon, 1992 (above)
PHOTOGRAPH BY ALLSPORT

Goran Ivanisevic, Wimbledon, 1995 (right)
PHOTOGRAPH BY CLIVE BRUNSKILL

*Ai Campionati di
Wimbledon, il più
tradizionale dei quattro
tornei, la superficie di
gioco è quella delle origini
e i campi erbosi vengono
mantenuti in condizioni
perfette per garantire
la continuità della
tradizionale atmosfera
inglese del Garden Party
del 1877.*

**Pete Sampras,
Wimbledon, 1995** (left)

**Ball-boy,
Wimbledon, 1995**
(right lower)
PHOTOGRAPHS BY CLIVE BRUNSKILL

**Net detail,
Wimbledon, 1995**
(right above)
PHOTOGRAPH BY GARY M PRIOR

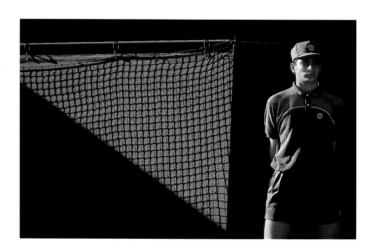

US Open

In keeping with its North American heritage, the US Open is the brashest of all the majors and brings the traditional annual Grand Slam circuit to its yearly conclusion. In its own way Flushing Meadows is a microcosm of New York life with its concrete, commercialism and noise, all of which helps establish its own individual style as epitomised by the fervour of the fans.

US Open, 1993

PHOTOGRAPH BY SIMON BRUTY

*Dans la lignée de son héritage nord-américain, l'US Open
est le plus impétueux de tous les principaux événements ,
et boucle le circuit traditionnel annuel du Grand Chelem.
Flushing Meadows est, à sa façon, un microcosme de la vie
new-yorkaise, avec son béton, son esprit commerçant
et son environnement bruyant. Chacun de cés élements
caractérise le style de cette ville, comme si la ferveur
de ses fans y était incarnée.*

Jana Novotna, US Open, 1991 (left)
PHOTOGRAPHS BY SIMON BRUTY

Gigi Fernandez, US Open, 1991 (above)
PHOTOGRAPH BY DAN SMITH

Den Abschluß findet der jährliche Grand Slam-Zirkus bei den US-Open, dem, entsprechend seiner nordamerikanischen Tradition, schillerndsten der vier großen Turniere. Auf seine eigene Art und Weise ist Flushing Meadows mit all seinem Beton, seinem Kommerz und seinem Lärm ein Mikrokosmos inmitten New Yorks mit einem ganz eigenen Stil, der sich in der Leidenschaft der Fans widerspiegelt.

*Haciendo honor a su
herencia norteamericana,
el Abierto de Estados
Unidos es el más
extravagante de los
grandes torneos,
y tradicionalmente la
última cita del circuito
anual del Grand Slam.
Flushing Meadows
puede considerarse un
microcosmos de la vida de
Nueva York: cemento,
ruido y mercantilismo
contribuyen a crear un
estilo individual,
sintetizado en la pasión
de los fans.*

**Michael Chang,
US Open, 1992** (left)

**Andre Agassi,
US Open, 1992** (right)

PHOTOGRAPHS BY SIMON BRUTY

Gli Open statunitensi, in armonia con la tradizione nord-americana,

sono i più trascinanti dei quattro più importanti tornei del mondo

e chiudono il tradizionale circuito annuale del Grande Slam.

L'ambiente di Flushing Meadows rispecchia perfettamente

la vita di New York, la sua concretezza, il business e il rumore;

il tutto conferisce uno stile assolutamente particolare

che ben si riassume nell'entusiasmo dei tifosi.

Monica Seles, US Open, 1995 (left)
PHOTOGRAPH BY GARY M PRIOR

Pete Sampras, US Open, 1995 (above)
PHOTOGRAPH BY SIMON BRUTY

POWERPLAY

Brenda Schultz-McCarthy, US Open, 1995

PHOTOGRAPH BY GARY M PRIOR

POWERPLAY

by Henry Wancke

THE MODERN SPORT OF TENNIS is but a distant relation to the original 1873 *Sphairistike* Victorian country garden game of Major Walter Clopton Wingfield.

These days the ball can be struck by a player's racket to speeds exceeding 130mph, so reflexes have to be extremely quick, players must have excellent hand-eye co-ordination for control and timing, plus the fitness of all-round athletes to survive struggles which could last well over three hours. And to the victor go the spoils of prize money, better computer ratings, plus increased public esteem and popularity.

From the safe haven of the stands, the public can readily witness the rising sap of adrenaline as two opponents prepare to confront each other. This gladiatorial struggle is a feature which applies to all sports, from the pugilistic brutality of boxing to the more seemly striking of a ball across a net. But it is the strength of the protagonists, whether through the power of their arm, the awareness of their minds, or even stamina, that spectators come to see.

Power tennis is the current order of the day.

Le TENNIS MODERNE s'est beaucoup éloigné du jeu pratiqué à l'origine, en 1873, dans les jardins victoriens, et inventé par le Major Walter Clopton Wingfield.

De nos jours, la balle peut être frappée par la raquette d'un joueur à des vitesses supérieures à 130 miles/heure. Les réflexes doivent de ce fait être extrêmement rapides, les joueurs doivent faire preuve d'une excellente coordination pour assurer le contrôle et la synchronisation de leur jeu. Ils doivent en outre avoir une excellente forme physique afin de survivre aux combats qui peuvent durer plus de trois heures. Le vainqueur se voit remettre de l'argent, améliore son classement mondial, fait progresser l'estime que le public a pour lui, et renforce sa popularité.

Assis confortablement, à l'abri dans les stands, le public est témoin de la montée d'adrénaline des deux adversaires sur le point de s'affronter. Cette lutte qui rappelle celle des gladiateurs est propre à toutes les rencontres sportives, depuis les combats brutaux et violents de boxe jusqu'aux échanges plus convenables de balles au-dessus du filet. Mais c'est avant tout la force des joueurs, la puissance de leurs bras, la rapidité de leur esprit, et même leur endurance que les spectateurs viennent voir.

La puissance du jeu est aujourd'hui de rigueur dans le tennis.

Michael Stich, US Open, 1994
("Powerplay", pages 106-107)
PHOTOGRAPH BY CLIVE BRUNSKILL

DAS MODERNE TENNIS hat nur noch wenig Ähnlichkeit mit dem ursprünglichen viktorianischen Gartenspiel von Major Walter Clopton Wingfield.

Bei Geschwindigkeiten von über 200 km/h, die ein hart geschlagener Tennisball heute erreichen kann, benötigen die Spieler heute nicht nur extrem schnelle Reflexe, sondern auch eine ausgezeichnete Koordination von Augen und Händen, um Ballkontrolle und richtiges Timing zu gewährleisten, sowie die körperliche Fitneß eines Allround-Athleten, um Spiele durchstehen zu können, die mitunter länger als drei Stunden dauern. Der Sieger wird dafür mit üppigen Preisgeldern, Punkten auf der Computer-Weltrangliste sowie öffentlichem Ansehen und Popularität belohnt.

Aus sicherer Entfernung können die Zuschauer beobachten, wie der Adrenalinspiegel bei den Kontrahenten auf dem Platz steigt. Dieser gladiatorengleiche Kampf ist allen Sportarten gemein und reicht von der faustkämpferischen Brutalität des Boxens bis zum gemäßigteren, über ein Netz ausgetragenen Schlagabtausch mit Hilfe von Tennisbällen. Letztendlich ist es aber diese Stärke der Protagonisten, die sich in der Kraft ihrer Arme, ihrer Geistesgegenwart oder ihrer Kondition offenbart, die die Zuschauer sehen wollen.

Wir leben heute in der Welt des „Power-Tennis".

EL TENIS MODERNO es un pariente lejano del Sphairistike, un juego inventado en 1873 por el Comandante Walter Clopton Wingfield que se desarrollaba en los jardines de las villas victorianas.

Hoy en día, la raqueta de un tenista puede impulsar la pelota a velocidades superiores a 200 km/h. Por eso el jugador debe tener una extraordinaria rapidez de reflejos, una excelente coordinación entre la muñeca y la vista para calibrar la fuerza y el tempo y, además, una impresionante forma física que le permita sobrevivir a combates que a veces duran más de tres horas. El vencedor se lleva el botín: premios en metálico, ascenso en la clasificación, aumento de la popularidad y de la estima del público...

Desde el seguro refugio de las gradas, los espectadores contemplan admirados cómo, a medida que se aproxima el inicio del partido, sube la adrenalina en los cuerpos de los contrincantes. Esta "lucha entre gladiadores" es un rasgo común a todos los deportes, desde la brutalidad del boxeo hasta el menos violento paso de la pelota de un lado a otro de la red. Pero lo que los espectadores desean ver es la fuerza de los protagonistas, ya se manifieste en la potencia de su brazo, en la concentración de su mente o en la pura resistencia física.

Lo que hoy interesa es el tenis-potencia.

IL TENNIS MODERNO ha ormai solo lontane analogie con l'originario gioco dello Sphairistike, lanciato dal Maggiore Walter Clopton Wingfield e che veniva giocato in epoca vittoriana nei giardini di campagna.

Ai giorni nostri una racchetta può colpire la palla ad una velocità di oltre 200 chilometri orari. Occorre quindi che i giocatori abbiano riflessi estremamente rapidi, un'eccellente coordinazione mano-occhio per il controllo e il tempismo ed una preparazione atletica completa che permetta di poter sostenere incontri che possono durare anche ben più di tre ore. E al vincitore va il premio in denaro, un avanzamento della posizione in classifica e una maggior stima e popolarità presso il pubblico.

Anche il pubblico sugli spalti percepisce immediatamente l'aumento di adrenalina nel momento in cui due avversari si preparano all'incontro. Questa lotta fra gladiatori è una caratteristica tipica di tutti gli sport, dal brutale pugilato al meno rude mandare una palla oltre una rete. Ma è la forza dei protagonisti espressa dalla potenza del braccio, dalla lucidità mentale ed anche dalla loro resistenza che gli spettatori amano vedere.

Il tennis di oggi è ormai un tennis di potenza.

Henry Wancke is a freelance tennis writer and editor of Serve and Volley Magazine

Jeremy Bates, Wimbledon, 1994

PHOTOGRAPH BY GARY M PRIOR

*M*ore power to the tennis
elbow has been provided
by modern technology
producing rackets which,
when wielded with perfect
timing, can shoot
projectiles all over the
court! The talented player,
however, can keep it
in play.

Monica Seles,
Australian Open, 1993
PHOTOGRAPH BY SIMON BRUTY

La technologie moderne permet aux joueurs d'avoir une frappe plus puissante. Si le jeu est parfaitement synchronisé, la raquette peut projeter la balle d'un bout à l'autre du court. Cependant, le joueur de talent est à même de garder le contrôle de le balle adverse.

**Boris Becker,
Wimbledon, 1989**
(left above)
PHOTOGRAPH BY SIMON BRUTY

**Boris Becker,
French Open, 1991**
(left below)
PHOTOGRAPH BY CHRIS COLE

**Boris Becker,
Wimbledon, 1995** (right)
PHOTOGRAPH BY CLIVE BRUNSKILL

*Mit Hilfe neuer
Technologien wurden
Schläger entwickelt,
die, wenn sie richtig
geschwungen werden,
einen Ball wie ein
Geschoß über den
gesamten Platz befördern
können! Ein talentierter
Spieler hält den Ball
jedoch auch mit dem
schnellsten Schläger
im Spiel.*

**Kimiko Date,
US Open, 1993** (left)
PHOTOGRAPH BY SIMON BRUTY

**Jim Courier, Australian
Open, 1995**
PHOTOGRAPH BY CLIVE BRUNSKILL

*La tecnología moderna ha permitido fabricar raquetas
que aumentan la potencia del brazo del tenista. Cuando estos
instrumentos se acoplan ajustando perfectamente el tiempo,
pueden disparar auténticos proyectiles al otro extremo de la pista.
Sin embargo, los jugadores con talento son capaces
de controlar el juego.*

Goran Ivanisevic, Australian Open, 1994 (above)
PHOTOGRAPH BY CLIVE BRUNSKILL

Luke Jensen, US Open, 1995 (right)
PHOTOGRAPH BY GARY M PRIOR

E' la moderna tecnologia che fornisce più potenza al gomito del tennista, grazie a racchette che, controllate con perfetto tempismo, possono lanciare proiettili in ogni parte del campo... ma il bravo giocatore riesce comunque a mantenerla in gioco!

Marcelo Rios, US Open, 1995 (left)
PHOTOGRAPH BY SIMON BRUTY

Greg Rusedski, Wimbledon, 1995 (right)
PHOTOGRAPH BY GARY M PRIOR

IT'S ONLY A GAME...

Jana Novotna and Arantxa Sanchez Vicario, Wimbledon, 1995

PHOTOGRAPH BY CLIVE BRUNSKILL

IT'S ONLY A GAME...

by Clive Brunskill

THERE IS A TENDENCY to forget that tennis is only a game. But whilst the commitment of the players is a tribute to their professionalism and their clashes with authority always provide good entertainment and dramatic pictures, the original Corinthian characteristics of the players would seem to have been completely eradicated.

However, away from the daily pursuit of computer points, players still show human qualities when, for instance, they share the joy of victory or the pain of disappointment with a doubles partner or team-mate. That act, and a player's acknowledgement of a good shot, are features which are usually more than well received by spectators, as are the rare instances of good sportsmanship.

Those moments bring back memories of the swashbuckling days of the amateur sportsman who was as much at home on court swinging a racket, as he was in a lounge swigging a cocktail! Then of course, tennis was considered very much a part of the middle-class social life, as illustrated by the immortal 'anyone for tennis' phrase in George Bernard Shaw's 'Misadventure'. Tennis courts were de riguer then, not just private practice areas for the professional player!

On a TENDANCE à oublier que le tennis n'est qu'un jeu. Les caractéristiques corinthiennes du jeu d'origine ont disparu, même si aujourd'hui l'engagement des joueùrs témoigne de leur professionalisme, même si leur affrontement avec les arbitres donne un côté dramatique et divertissant aux matches. Toutefois, hormis leur obsession quotidienne à gagner des points dans le classement mondial, les joueurs font encors preuve de qualités humaines lorsqu'ils partagent, par exemple la joie d'une victoire ou la déception d'une défaite avec un partenaire de double ou un coéquipier. Cette réaction, ainsi que la reconnaissance de la part d'un joueur d'un bon coup de son adversaire sont généralement fort appréciées par les spectateurs, tout comme l'est la manifestation rare d'un excellent esprit sportif.

Ces moments rappellent les jours héroïques des sportifs amateurs qui se sentaient à l'aise sur un court tout autant que dans un salon. A l'époque, bien sûr, le tennis faisait partie intégrante de la vie sociale de la classe moyenne, ainsi que l'illustre l'expression éternelle de George Bernard Shaw "le tennis pour tous" dans son ouvrage 'Misadventure'. La fréquentation des courts de tennis était alors de rigueur, Les courts n'étaient pas que des terrains privés d'entraînement réservés aux professionnels!

Ivan Lendl, French Open, 1986
("It's Only a Game…", pages 122-123)
PHOTOGRAPH BY SIMON BRUTY

MAN VERGIßT MANCHMAL, daß Tennis letztendlich doch nur ein Spiel ist. Bei allem Engagement der Spieler, das eher als Tribut an ihre Professionalität zu sehen ist, und bei all ihren Auseinandersetzungen mit der Autorität der Schiedsrichter, die immer wieder recht unterhaltsam sind und uns dramatische Bilder liefern, so scheinen doch die ursprünglichen korinthischen Wesensmerkmale der Spieler heute komplett vergessen.

Fernab von der täglichen Jagd nach ATP-Punkten zeigen sich aber auch heute noch die menschlichen Qualitäten der Spieler, wenn sie die Freude nach einem Sieg oder auch die Enttäuschung nach einer Niederlage mit einem Doppelpartner oder einem Teamkollegen teilen. Solche Bilder, ebenso wie die Freude eines Spielers über einen guten Ball, werden von den Zuschauern ebenso honoriert wie die seltenen Augenblicke sportlicher Fairneß.

Diese Momente rufen Erinnerungen an die Zeiten der draufgängerischen Amateursportler wach, die den Tennisschläger auf dem Platz ebenso gerne und gekonnt schwangen wie das Cocktailglas in der Lounge. Zu dieser Zeit gehörte Tennis einfach zum gesellschaftlichen Leben der Mittelklasse, und der Tennisplatz war ein unerläßlicher Treffpunkt der Gesellschaft und nicht nur ein privates Trainingsgelände für Profi-Spieler.

CON FRECUENCIA se olvida que el tenis no es más que un juego. Pero mientras la entrega de los tenistas es consecuencia de su profesionalidad y sus enfrentamientos con los árbitros constituyen siempre motivo de entretenimiento y de fotos impactantes, parece que el original espíritu corintio de los jugadores ha sido completamente erradicado.

Sin embargo, además de la diaria persecución de los puntos para subir en la clasificación, los tenistas siguen mostrando cualidades humanas, como cuando comparten la alegría de la victoria o el dolor de la desilusión con un compañero de dobles o un miembro de su equipo. Esto y el reconocimiento por parte del tenista de un buen golpe, son rasgos que los espectadores reciben normalmente con agrado, al igual que los no muy frecuentes ejemplos de deportividad.

Esos momentos evocan los despreocupados días de los deportistas aficionados que manejaban la raqueta en la pista con igual soltura que los cócteles en el salón. Claro que entonces el tenis era considerado parte importante de la vida social de la clase media, como lo refleja la inmortal frase "¿Venís a jugar al tenis?" que aparece en 'Misadventure', de George Bernard Shaw. Las pistas de tenis formaban entonces parte de la etiqueta social, y no eran simplemente espacios para la práctica privada del tenista profesional.

C'È LA TENDENZA a dimenticare che il tennis sia solo un gioco. Ma se l'impegno dei giocatori è un tributo alla loro professionalità e le loro discussioni con i giudici sono sempre fonte di spettacolo e di immagini intense, l'originaria raffinatezza dei giocatori sembrerebbe essere ormai completamente scomparsa.

Tuttavia, indipendentemente dalla quotidiana scalata alla classifica, i giocatori mostrano ancora le loro qualità umane quando ad esempio condividono con il partner del doppio o un compagno di squadra l'emozione della vittoria o l'amarezza della sconfitta. Quei gesti e il compiacimento per un bel colpo espressi dai giocatori sono graditissimi agli spettatori perché rappresentano splendidi esempi di autentica sportività.

Quei momenti riportano alla memoria i gloriosi giorni dei gentlemen di un tempo che come sul campo di casa impugnavano la racchetta, così sorseggiavano un cocktail in un salotto. Naturalmente il tennis allora era considerato una consuetudine nella vita sociale della classe media, come ben testimonia l'immortale frase "tutti al tennis" nella commedia di George Bernard Shaw, 'Misadventure'. Praticare il tennis era allora un "must" e i campi non erano solo delle aree di allenamento riservate ai professionisti!

Clive Brunskill is a Staff photographer
for Allsport Photographic

Jana Novotna consoled by the Duchess of Kent, Wimbledon, 1993
PHOTOGRAPH BY CHRIS COLE

For millions of people around the world, tennis is only a game, a hobby, a means of keeping fit whilst pursuing social intercourse. At the other end of the spectrum it is big business for the few thousands who have dedicated their lives to playing tennis for their daily bread!

Boris Becker, French Open, 1989 (left)
<small>PHOTOGRAPH BY BOB MARTIN</small>

John McEnroe, Wimbledon, 1980 (below)
<small>PHOTOGRAPH BY STEVE POWELL</small>

Pour des millions de personnes dans le monde, le tennis n'est qu'un jeu,
un hobby, un moyen de
rester en forme tout en
entretenant des relations
sociales. A l'autre bout
du spectre, il s'agit
d'une véritable activité
commerciale pour les
quelques milliers qui ont
dédié leur vie au tennis
afin de gagner leur
pain quotidien !

Stefan Edberg,
Wimbledon, 1991 (left)
PHOTOGRAPH BY ALLSPORT

Goran Ivanisevic,
Italian Open, 1995 (right)
PHOTOGRAPH BY ANTON WANT

Für Millionen von Menschen überall in der Welt ist Tennis nichts weiter als ein Spiel, ein Hobby, eine Möglichkeit, sich im Kreise netter Menschen fit zu halten. Für die wenigen Tausend, die mit Tennisspielen ihren Lebensunterhalt verdienen, ist es auch ein großes Geschäft.

Petr Korda, Munich, 1993 (above)
PHOTOGRAPH BY CLIVE BRUNSKILL

Henri Leconte, French Open, 1992 (right)
PHOTOGRAPH BY CHRIS COLE

Germany, Davis Cup Final, 1993 (top)

Pete Sampras, Australian Open, 1995 (above)

Steffi Graf, Wimbledon, 1995 (right)

Photographs by Gary M Prior

John McEnroe,
Wimbledon, 1991 (above)
PHOTOGRAPH BY SIMON BRUTY

Jim Courier,
French Open, 1991 (right)
PHOTOGRAPH BY PASCAL RONDEAU

*Para millones de personas
de todo el mundo, el tenis
no es más que un juego,
una afición, un modo
de mantenerse en forma y
llevar, al mismo tiempo,
vida social. Pero también
es el polo opuesto:
un negocio extraordinario para unos pocos miles de personas que han dedicado sus vidas a jugar al tenis para ganarse el sustento.*

**Renae Stubbs,
Federation Cup, 1993** (right)

**Andrei Medvedev,
Wimbledon, 1994** (far right)

*Per milioni di persone nel mondo,
il tennis è solo un gioco,
un passatempo, un modo per
tenersi in forma e nello stesso
tempo mantenere delle relazioni
sociali. E' invece un grande
business per alcune migliaia di
persone che hanno dedicato la
loro vita al tennis proprio
perché quello è il loro lavoro!*

**Arantxa Sanchez Vicario,
Wimbledon, 1995** (far left above)

**Pete Sampras,
US Open, 1994** (far left below)
PHOTOGRAPHS BY CLIVE BRUNSKILL

**Martina Hingis,
Wimbledon, 1995** (left)

**Anke Huber,
Wimbledon, 1995** (right)
PHOTOGRAPHS BY GARY M PRIOR

Michael Chang,
French Open, 1994

PHOTOGRAPH BY CLIVE BRUNSKILL

The Jensen brothers, 1995 (left)

PHOTOGRAPH BY SIMON BRUTY

Mats Wilander, US Open, 1987 (below)

PHOTOGRAPH BY CHRIS COLE

Visions of Tennis

The photographs in this book have been selected from the
extensive tennis library of Allsport, the world's leading sports picture agency.
The photographs and their availability in all corners of the world
would not have been possible without the help of the following:
The Photographers, Picture Researchers, Darkroom Staff,
Picture Desk Operators, Accounts Staff, Clerical Staff
and everyone else in the Allsport offices at

ALLSPORT UK
3 Greenlea Park
Prince George's Road
London SW19 2JD

Tel: (0181) 685 1010 • Fax: (0181) 648 5240

ALLSPORT USA
Sunset Coast Plaza, Suite A300,
17383 Sunset Boulevard,
Pacific Palisades,
California 90272

Tel: (310) 230 3400 • Fax: (310) 573 7600

ALLSPORT NEW YORK
13B Gramercy Place
280 Park Avenue South
New York 10010

Tel: (212) 979 0903 • Fax: (212) 979 0460

and the international network of agencies
on all five continents.

Quiller Press Ltd
46 Lillie Road, London SW6 1TN

Tel: 0171 499 6529 • Fax: 0171 381 8941